RuMi Art Design 2022

No part of this book may be reproduced in any form without permission in writing from the author.

RuMi Art Design
Email: rumiart@proton.me

Published by: RuMi Art Design

Writing, Editing & Design by RuMi Art Design

Printed in Australia

ISBN 978-0-646-86448-8

Scriptures taken from the Holy Bible, New International Version®, NIV®. Copyright © 1973, 1978, 1984, 2011 by Biblica, Inc.™ Used by permission of Zondervan. All rights reserved worldwide. www.zondervan.com The "NIV" and "New International Version" are trademarks registered in the United States Patent and Trademark Office by Biblica, Inc.™

Hello friend,

This journal was designed and created for those of us that need or want a little guidance, but also space to write freely.

The prompts can be used any time of the day. You might want to jot down a scripture, a characteristic of God, or something from the day that brought you to God e.g. a timely word from someone, or a beautiful sunset. Prayer requests and answers show us God's faithfulness and provision, and gratitude opens our hearts to Him.

The free space is for whatever you want to write. Some suggestions - a significant dream, a letter from God to you, something that is on your heart and mind.

I hope you enjoy using this journal and that it brings you closer to God.

RuMi

This is the confidence we have in approaching God: that if we ask anything according to his will, he hears us.

1 John 5:14

5 minute journaling

ONE THING I WANT TO THINK/REMEMBER ABOUT TODAY...

___

PRAYER REQUESTS AND ANSWERS

___

TODAY I'M GRATEFUL FOR...

___

Date_____

5 minute journaling

ONE THING I WANT TO THINK/REMEMBER ABOUT TODAY...

_____
_____
_____
_____
_____
_____

PRAYER REQUESTS AND ANSWERS

_____
_____
_____
_____
_____
_____

TODAY I'M GRATEFUL FOR...

_____
_____
_____
_____
_____
_____

Date_____

5 minute journaling

ONE THING I WANT TO THINK/REMEMBER ABOUT TODAY...

_____
_____
_____
_____
_____

PRAYER REQUESTS AND ANSWERS

_____
_____
_____
_____
_____

TODAY I'M GRATEFUL FOR...

_____
_____
_____
_____
_____

Date_____

5 minute journaling

ONE THING I WANT TO THINK/REMEMBER ABOUT TODAY...

_____
_____
_____
_____
_____
_____

PRAYER REQUESTS AND ANSWERS

_____
_____
_____
_____
_____
_____

TODAY I'M GRATEFUL FOR...

_____
_____
_____
_____
_____
_____

Date_____

5 minute journaling

ONE THING I WANT TO THINK/REMEMBER ABOUT TODAY...

_____
_____
_____
_____
_____

PRAYER REQUESTS AND ANSWERS

_____
_____
_____
_____
_____

TODAY I'M GRATEFUL FOR...

_____
_____
_____
_____
_____

Date_____

What's on your heart

Date_____

Date_____

Then you will call on me
and come and pray to me,
and I will listen to you.
Jeremiah 29:12

5 minute journaling

ONE THING I WANT TO THINK/REMEMBER ABOUT TODAY...

PRAYER REQUESTS AND ANSWERS

TODAY I'M GRATEFUL FOR...

Date_____

5 minute journaling

ONE THING I WANT TO THINK/REMEMBER ABOUT TODAY...
___
___
___
___
___
___

PRAYER REQUESTS AND ANSWERS
___
___
___
___
___
___

TODAY I'M GRATEFUL FOR...
___
___
___
___
___
___

Date_____

5 minute journaling

ONE THING I WANT TO THINK/REMEMBER ABOUT TODAY...

_____
_____
_____
_____
_____
_____

PRAYER REQUESTS AND ANSWERS

_____
_____
_____
_____
_____

TODAY I'M GRATEFUL FOR...

_____
_____
_____
_____
_____

Date_____

ONE THING I WANT TO THINK/REMEMBER ABOUT TODAY...

PRAYER REQUESTS AND ANSWERS

TODAY I'M GRATEFUL FOR...

Date_____

5 minute journaling

ONE THING I WANT TO THINK/REMEMBER ABOUT TODAY...

_____
_____
_____
_____
_____
_____

PRAYER REQUESTS AND ANSWERS

_____
_____
_____
_____
_____
_____

TODAY I'M GRATEFUL FOR...

_____
_____
_____
_____
_____
_____

Date_____

What's on your heart

_____

_____

_____

_____

_____

_____

_____

_____

_____

_____

_____

_____

_____

_____

_____

_____

_____

Date_____

Date_____

And pray in the Spirit on all
occasions with all kinds of prayers
and requests. With this in mind,
be alert and always keep on
praying for all the Lord's people.
Ephesians 6:18

5 minute journaling

ONE THING I WANT TO THINK/REMEMBER ABOUT TODAY...

_____
_____
_____
_____
_____
_____

PRAYER REQUESTS AND ANSWERS

_____
_____
_____
_____
_____
_____

TODAY I'M GRATEFUL FOR...

_____
_____
_____
_____
_____
_____

Date_____

5 minute journaling

ONE THING I WANT TO THINK/REMEMBER ABOUT TODAY...

_____
_____
_____
_____
_____
_____

PRAYER REQUESTS AND ANSWERS

_____
_____
_____
_____
_____
_____

TODAY I'M GRATEFUL FOR...

_____
_____
_____
_____
_____
_____

Date_____

5 minute journaling

ONE THING I WANT TO THINK/REMEMBER ABOUT TODAY...

_____
_____
_____
_____
_____

PRAYER REQUESTS AND ANSWERS

_____
_____
_____
_____
_____

TODAY I'M GRATEFUL FOR...

_____
_____
_____
_____
_____

Date_____

5 minute journaling

ONE THING I WANT TO THINK/REMEMBER ABOUT TODAY...

_____
_____
_____
_____
_____
_____

PRAYER REQUESTS AND ANSWERS

_____
_____
_____
_____
_____
_____

TODAY I'M GRATEFUL FOR...

_____
_____
_____
_____
_____
_____

Date_____

ONE THING I WANT TO THINK/REMEMBER ABOUT TODAY...

_____
_____
_____
_____
_____
_____

PRAYER REQUESTS AND ANSWERS

_____
_____
_____
_____
_____
_____

TODAY I'M GRATEFUL FOR...

_____
_____
_____
_____
_____
_____

Date_____

What's on your heart

Date _____

Date_____

Is anyone among you in trouble?
Let them pray. Is anyone happy?
Let them sing songs of praise.
James 5:13

5 minute journaling

ONE THING I WANT TO THINK/REMEMBER ABOUT TODAY...

_____
_____
_____
_____
_____
_____

PRAYER REQUESTS AND ANSWERS

_____
_____
_____
_____
_____
_____

TODAY I'M GRATEFUL FOR...

_____
_____
_____
_____
_____
_____

Date_____

ONE THING I WANT TO THINK/REMEMBER ABOUT TODAY...

_____
_____
_____
_____
_____

PRAYER REQUESTS AND ANSWERS

_____
_____
_____
_____
_____
_____

TODAY I'M GRATEFUL FOR...

_____
_____
_____
_____
_____

Date_____

5 minute journaling

ONE THING I WANT TO THINK/REMEMBER ABOUT TODAY...

_____
_____
_____
_____
_____

PRAYER REQUESTS AND ANSWERS

_____
_____
_____
_____
_____

TODAY I'M GRATEFUL FOR...

_____
_____
_____
_____
_____

Date_____

ONE THING I WANT TO THINK/REMEMBER ABOUT TODAY...

___
___
___
___
___
___

PRAYER REQUESTS AND ANSWERS

___
___
___
___
___
___

TODAY I'M GRATEFUL FOR...

___
___
___
___
___
___

Date_____

5 minute journaling

ONE THING I WANT TO THINK/REMEMBER ABOUT TODAY...

_____
_____
_____
_____
_____

PRAYER REQUESTS AND ANSWERS

_____
_____
_____
_____
_____

TODAY I'M GRATEFUL FOR...

_____
_____
_____
_____
_____

Date_____

What's on your heart

Date_____

Date_____

Therefore I tell you, whatever you ask for in prayer, believe that you have received it, and it will be yours.
Mark 11:24

ONE THING I WANT TO THINK/REMEMBER ABOUT TODAY...

PRAYER REQUESTS AND ANSWERS

TODAY I'M GRATEFUL FOR...

Date_____

5 minute journaling

ONE THING I WANT TO THINK/REMEMBER ABOUT TODAY...

_____
_____
_____
_____
_____
_____

PRAYER REQUESTS AND ANSWERS

_____
_____
_____
_____
_____
_____

TODAY I'M GRATEFUL FOR...

_____
_____
_____
_____
_____
_____

Date_____

ONE THING I WANT TO THINK/REMEMBER ABOUT TODAY...

_____
_____
_____
_____
_____
_____

PRAYER REQUESTS AND ANSWERS

_____
_____
_____
_____
_____
_____

TODAY I'M GRATEFUL FOR...

_____
_____
_____
_____
_____
_____

Date_____

5 minute journaling

ONE THING I WANT TO THINK/REMEMBER ABOUT TODAY...

_____
_____
_____
_____
_____

PRAYER REQUESTS AND ANSWERS

_____
_____
_____
_____
_____

TODAY I'M GRATEFUL FOR...

_____
_____
_____
_____
_____

Date_____

5 minute journaling

ONE THING I WANT TO THINK/REMEMBER ABOUT TODAY...

PRAYER REQUESTS AND ANSWERS

TODAY I'M GRATEFUL FOR...

Date_____

What's on your heart

Date_____

Date_____

In the same way, the Spirit helps us in our weakness. We do not know what we ought to pray for, but the Spirit himself intercedes for us through wordless groans.
Romans 8:26

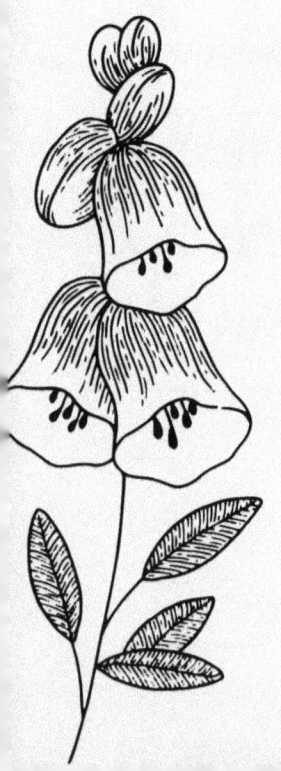

5 minute journaling

ONE THING I WANT TO THINK/REMEMBER ABOUT TODAY...

_____
_____
_____
_____
_____
_____

PRAYER REQUESTS AND ANSWERS

_____
_____
_____
_____
_____
_____

TODAY I'M GRATEFUL FOR...

_____
_____
_____
_____
_____
_____

Date_____

5 minute journaling

ONE THING I WANT TO THINK/REMEMBER ABOUT TODAY...

_____
_____
_____
_____
_____

PRAYER REQUESTS AND ANSWERS

_____
_____
_____
_____
_____

TODAY I'M GRATEFUL FOR...

_____
_____
_____
_____
_____

Date_____

5 minute journaling

ONE THING I WANT TO THINK/REMEMBER ABOUT TODAY...

PRAYER REQUESTS AND ANSWERS

TODAY I'M GRATEFUL FOR...

Date_____

ONE THING I WANT TO THINK/REMEMBER ABOUT TODAY...

PRAYER REQUESTS AND ANSWERS

TODAY I'M GRATEFUL FOR...

Date_____

5 minute journaling

ONE THING I WANT TO THINK/REMEMBER ABOUT TODAY...

_____
_____
_____
_____
_____

PRAYER REQUESTS AND ANSWERS

_____
_____
_____
_____
_____

TODAY I'M GRATEFUL FOR...

_____
_____
_____
_____
_____

Date_____

What's on your heart

_____
_____
_____
_____
_____
_____
_____
_____
_____
_____
_____
_____
_____
_____
_____
_____
_____
_____
_____

Date_____

Date_____

I call on you, my God, for you will answer me, turn your ear to me and hear my prayer.
Psalms 17:6

5 minute journaling

ONE THING I WANT TO THINK/REMEMBER ABOUT TODAY...

___

PRAYER REQUESTS AND ANSWERS

___

TODAY I'M GRATEFUL FOR...

___

Date_____

5 minute journaling

ONE THING I WANT TO THINK/REMEMBER ABOUT TODAY...

_____
_____
_____
_____
_____

PRAYER REQUESTS AND ANSWERS

_____
_____
_____
_____
_____
_____

TODAY I'M GRATEFUL FOR...

_____
_____
_____
_____
_____

Date_____

5 minute journaling

ONE THING I WANT TO THINK/REMEMBER ABOUT TODAY...

_____
_____
_____
_____
_____
_____

PRAYER REQUESTS AND ANSWERS

_____
_____
_____
_____
_____
_____

TODAY I'M GRATEFUL FOR...

_____
_____
_____
_____
_____
_____

Date_____

5 minute journaling

ONE THING I WANT TO THINK/REMEMBER ABOUT TODAY...

_____
_____
_____
_____
_____

PRAYER REQUESTS AND ANSWERS

_____
_____
_____
_____
_____

TODAY I'M GRATEFUL FOR...

_____
_____
_____
_____
_____

Date_____

5 minute journaling

ONE THING I WANT TO THINK/REMEMBER ABOUT TODAY...

___

PRAYER REQUESTS AND ANSWERS

___

TODAY I'M GRATEFUL FOR...

___

Date_____

What's on your heart

_____
_____
_____
_____
_____
_____
_____
_____
_____
_____
_____
_____
_____
_____
_____
_____
_____
_____
_____
_____

Date_____

Date_____

May my prayer be set before you like incense, may the lifting up of my hands be like the evening sacrifice.

Psalms 141:2

5 minute journaling

ONE THING I WANT TO THINK/REMEMBER ABOUT TODAY...

_____
_____
_____
_____
_____
_____

PRAYER REQUESTS AND ANSWERS

_____
_____
_____
_____
_____
_____

TODAY I'M GRATEFUL FOR...

_____
_____
_____
_____
_____
_____

Date_____

5 minute journaling

ONE THING I WANT TO THINK/REMEMBER ABOUT TODAY...

_____
_____
_____
_____
_____
_____

PRAYER REQUESTS AND ANSWERS

_____
_____
_____
_____
_____
_____

TODAY I'M GRATEFUL FOR...

_____
_____
_____
_____
_____
_____

Date_____

5 minute journaling

ONE THING I WANT TO THINK/REMEMBER ABOUT TODAY...

_____
_____
_____
_____
_____
_____

PRAYER REQUESTS AND ANSWERS

_____
_____
_____
_____
_____
_____

TODAY I'M GRATEFUL FOR...

_____
_____
_____
_____
_____
_____

Date_____

5 minute journaling

ONE THING I WANT TO THINK/REMEMBER ABOUT TODAY...
_____
_____
_____
_____
_____

PRAYER REQUESTS AND ANSWERS
_____
_____
_____
_____
_____

TODAY I'M GRATEFUL FOR...
_____
_____
_____
_____
_____

Date_____

5 minute journaling

ONE THING I WANT TO THINK/REMEMBER ABOUT TODAY...

_____
_____
_____
_____
_____

PRAYER REQUESTS AND ANSWERS

_____
_____
_____
_____
_____

TODAY I'M GRATEFUL FOR...

_____
_____
_____
_____
_____

Date_____

What's on your heart

Date_____

Date_____

But when you pray, go into your room, close the door and pray to your Father, who is unseen. Then your Father, who sees what is done in secret, will reward you.

                  Matthew 6:6

5 minute journaling

ONE THING I WANT TO THINK/REMEMBER ABOUT TODAY...

___

PRAYER REQUESTS AND ANSWERS

___

TODAY I'M GRATEFUL FOR...

___

Date_____

5 minute journaling

ONE THING I WANT TO THINK/REMEMBER ABOUT TODAY...

_____
_____
_____
_____
_____

PRAYER REQUESTS AND ANSWERS

_____
_____
_____
_____
_____

TODAY I'M GRATEFUL FOR...

_____
_____
_____
_____
_____

Date_____

5 minute journaling

ONE THING I WANT TO THINK/REMEMBER ABOUT TODAY...

_____
_____
_____
_____
_____

PRAYER REQUESTS AND ANSWERS

_____
_____
_____
_____
_____
_____

TODAY I'M GRATEFUL FOR...

_____
_____
_____
_____
_____
_____

Date_____

5 minute journaling

ONE THING I WANT TO THINK/REMEMBER ABOUT TODAY...

_____
_____
_____
_____
_____

PRAYER REQUESTS AND ANSWERS

_____
_____
_____
_____
_____

TODAY I'M GRATEFUL FOR...

_____
_____
_____
_____
_____

Date_____

5 minute journaling

ONE THING I WANT TO THINK/REMEMBER ABOUT TODAY...

_____
_____
_____
_____
_____

PRAYER REQUESTS AND ANSWERS

_____
_____
_____
_____
_____

TODAY I'M GRATEFUL FOR...

_____
_____
_____
_____
_____

Date_____

What's on your heart

_____
_____
_____
_____
_____
_____
_____
_____
_____
_____
_____
_____
_____
_____
_____
_____
_____

Date_____

Date_____

Answer me when I call to you, my righteous God. Give me relief from my distress, have mercy on me and hear my prayer.
Psalms 4:1

5 minute journaling

ONE THING I WANT TO THINK/REMEMBER ABOUT TODAY...

_____
_____
_____
_____
_____
_____

PRAYER REQUESTS AND ANSWERS

_____
_____
_____
_____
_____
_____

TODAY I'M GRATEFUL FOR...

_____
_____
_____
_____
_____
_____

Date_____

5 minute journaling

ONE THING I WANT TO THINK/REMEMBER ABOUT TODAY...

_____
_____
_____
_____
_____
_____

PRAYER REQUESTS AND ANSWERS

_____
_____
_____
_____
_____
_____

TODAY I'M GRATEFUL FOR...

_____
_____
_____
_____
_____
_____

Date_____

5 minute journaling

ONE THING I WANT TO THINK/REMEMBER ABOUT TODAY...

_____
_____
_____
_____
_____

PRAYER REQUESTS AND ANSWERS

_____
_____
_____
_____
_____

TODAY I'M GRATEFUL FOR...

_____
_____
_____
_____
_____

Date_____

ONE THING I WANT TO THINK/REMEMBER ABOUT TODAY...

_____
_____
_____
_____
_____
_____

PRAYER REQUESTS AND ANSWERS

_____
_____
_____
_____
_____
_____

TODAY I'M GRATEFUL FOR...

_____
_____
_____
_____
_____
_____

Date_____

5 minute journaling

ONE THING I WANT TO THINK/REMEMBER ABOUT TODAY...

_____
_____
_____
_____
_____
_____

PRAYER REQUESTS AND ANSWERS

_____
_____
_____
_____
_____
_____

TODAY I'M GRATEFUL FOR...

_____
_____
_____
_____
_____
_____

Date_____

What's on your heart

Date_____

Date_____

But I tell you, love your enemies
and pray for those who persecute you
Matthew 5:44

ONE THING I WANT TO THINK/REMEMBER ABOUT TODAY...
_____
_____
_____
_____
_____

PRAYER REQUESTS AND ANSWERS
_____
_____
_____
_____
_____

TODAY I'M GRATEFUL FOR...
_____
_____
_____
_____
_____

Date_____

5 minute journaling

ONE THING I WANT TO THINK/REMEMBER ABOUT TODAY...

_____
_____
_____
_____
_____

PRAYER REQUESTS AND ANSWERS

_____
_____
_____
_____
_____

TODAY I'M GRATEFUL FOR...

_____
_____
_____
_____
_____

Date_____

5 minute journaling

ONE THING I WANT TO THINK/REMEMBER ABOUT TODAY...

_____
_____
_____
_____
_____

PRAYER REQUESTS AND ANSWERS

_____
_____
_____
_____
_____

TODAY I'M GRATEFUL FOR...

_____
_____
_____
_____
_____

Date_____

5 minute journaling

ONE THING I WANT TO THINK/REMEMBER ABOUT TODAY...

_____
_____
_____
_____
_____
_____

PRAYER REQUESTS AND ANSWERS

_____
_____
_____
_____
_____
_____

TODAY I'M GRATEFUL FOR...

_____
_____
_____
_____
_____
_____

Date_____

ONE THING I WANT TO THINK/REMEMBER ABOUT TODAY...

_____
_____
_____
_____
_____

PRAYER REQUESTS AND ANSWERS

_____
_____
_____
_____
_____

TODAY I'M GRATEFUL FOR...

_____
_____
_____
_____
_____

Date_____

What's on your heart

_____
_____
_____
_____
_____
_____
_____
_____
_____
_____
_____
_____
_____
_____
_____
_____
_____

Date_____

Date_____

Do not be anxious about anything,
but in every situation, by prayer
and petition, with thanksgiving,
present your requests to God.
Philippians 4:6

5 minute journaling

ONE THING I WANT TO THINK/REMEMBER ABOUT TODAY...

___

PRAYER REQUESTS AND ANSWERS

___

TODAY I'M GRATEFUL FOR...

___

Date_____

5 minute journaling

ONE THING I WANT TO THINK/REMEMBER ABOUT TODAY...

_____
_____
_____
_____
_____

PRAYER REQUESTS AND ANSWERS

_____
_____
_____
_____
_____

TODAY I'M GRATEFUL FOR...

_____
_____
_____
_____
_____

Date_____

5 minute journaling

ONE THING I WANT TO THINK/REMEMBER ABOUT TODAY...

_____
_____
_____
_____
_____

PRAYER REQUESTS AND ANSWERS

_____
_____
_____
_____
_____

TODAY I'M GRATEFUL FOR...

_____
_____
_____
_____
_____

Date_____

ONE THING I WANT TO THINK/REMEMBER ABOUT TODAY...

_____
_____
_____
_____
_____

PRAYER REQUESTS AND ANSWERS

_____
_____
_____
_____
_____

TODAY I'M GRATEFUL FOR...

_____
_____
_____
_____
_____

Date_____

5 minute journaling

ONE THING I WANT TO THINK/REMEMBER ABOUT TODAY...

_____
_____
_____
_____
_____
_____

PRAYER REQUESTS AND ANSWERS

_____
_____
_____
_____
_____
_____

TODAY I'M GRATEFUL FOR...

_____
_____
_____
_____
_____
_____

Date_____

What's on your heart

Date_____

Date_____

Call to me and I will answer you
and tell you great and unsearchable
things you do not know.
Jeremiah 33:3

5 minute journaling

ONE THING I WANT TO THINK/REMEMBER ABOUT TODAY...

_____
_____
_____
_____
_____

PRAYER REQUESTS AND ANSWERS

_____
_____
_____
_____
_____

TODAY I'M GRATEFUL FOR...

_____
_____
_____
_____
_____

Date_____

5 minute journaling

ONE THING I WANT TO THINK/REMEMBER ABOUT TODAY...

_____
_____
_____
_____
_____

PRAYER REQUESTS AND ANSWERS

_____
_____
_____
_____
_____
_____

TODAY I'M GRATEFUL FOR...

_____
_____
_____
_____
_____
_____

Date_____

5 minute journaling

ONE THING I WANT TO THINK/REMEMBER ABOUT TODAY...

___
___
___
___
___
___

PRAYER REQUESTS AND ANSWERS

___
___
___
___
___
___

TODAY I'M GRATEFUL FOR...

___
___
___
___
___
___

Date_____

5 minute journaling

ONE THING I WANT TO THINK/REMEMBER ABOUT TODAY...

_____
_____
_____
_____
_____
_____

PRAYER REQUESTS AND ANSWERS

_____
_____
_____
_____
_____
_____

TODAY I'M GRATEFUL FOR...

_____
_____
_____
_____
_____
_____

Date_____

ONE THING I WANT TO THINK/REMEMBER ABOUT TODAY...

_____
_____
_____
_____
_____

PRAYER REQUESTS AND ANSWERS

_____
_____
_____
_____
_____

TODAY I'M GRATEFUL FOR...

_____
_____
_____
_____
_____

Date_____

What's on your heart

_____
_____
_____
_____
_____
_____
_____
_____
_____
_____
_____
_____
_____
_____
_____
_____
_____
_____

Date_____

Date_____

Therefore confess your sins to each other and pray for each other so that you may be healed. The prayer of a righteous person is powerful and effective.

James 5:16

5 minute journaling

ONE THING I WANT TO THINK/REMEMBER ABOUT TODAY...

_____
_____
_____
_____
_____
_____

PRAYER REQUESTS AND ANSWERS

_____
_____
_____
_____
_____
_____

TODAY I'M GRATEFUL FOR...

_____
_____
_____
_____
_____
_____

Date_____

# 5 minute journaling

ONE THING I WANT TO THINK/REMEMBER ABOUT TODAY...

_____
_____
_____
_____
_____

PRAYER REQUESTS AND ANSWERS

_____
_____
_____
_____
_____

TODAY I'M GRATEFUL FOR...

_____
_____
_____
_____
_____

Date_____

5 minute journaling

ONE THING I WANT TO THINK/REMEMBER ABOUT TODAY...

_____
_____
_____
_____
_____

PRAYER REQUESTS AND ANSWERS

_____
_____
_____
_____
_____

TODAY I'M GRATEFUL FOR...

_____
_____
_____
_____
_____

Date_____

ONE THING I WANT TO THINK/REMEMBER ABOUT TODAY...

_____
_____
_____
_____
_____

PRAYER REQUESTS AND ANSWERS

_____
_____
_____
_____
_____

TODAY I'M GRATEFUL FOR...

_____
_____
_____
_____
_____

Date_____

5 minute journaling

ONE THING I WANT TO THINK/REMEMBER ABOUT TODAY...

_____
_____
_____
_____
_____
_____

PRAYER REQUESTS AND ANSWERS

_____
_____
_____
_____
_____
_____

TODAY I'M GRATEFUL FOR...

_____
_____
_____
_____
_____
_____

Date_____

What's on your heart

Date_____

Date_____

Devote yourselves to prayer, being watchful and thankful.

Colossians 4:2

ONE THING I WANT TO THINK/REMEMBER ABOUT TODAY...

PRAYER REQUESTS AND ANSWERS

TODAY I'M GRATEFUL FOR...

Date_____

5 minute journaling

ONE THING I WANT TO THINK/REMEMBER ABOUT TODAY...

_____
_____
_____
_____
_____

PRAYER REQUESTS AND ANSWERS

_____
_____
_____
_____
_____

TODAY I'M GRATEFUL FOR...

_____
_____
_____
_____
_____

Date_____

ONE THING I WANT TO THINK/REMEMBER ABOUT TODAY...

_____
_____
_____
_____
_____

PRAYER REQUESTS AND ANSWERS

_____
_____
_____
_____
_____

TODAY I'M GRATEFUL FOR...

_____
_____
_____
_____
_____

Date_____

5 minute journaling

ONE THING I WANT TO THINK/REMEMBER ABOUT TODAY...

_____
_____
_____
_____
_____
_____

PRAYER REQUESTS AND ANSWERS

_____
_____
_____
_____
_____
_____

TODAY I'M GRATEFUL FOR...

_____
_____
_____
_____
_____
_____

Date_____

 # 5 minute journaling

ONE THING I WANT TO THINK/REMEMBER ABOUT TODAY...

___

PRAYER REQUESTS AND ANSWERS

___

TODAY I'M GRATEFUL FOR...

___

Date_____

What's on your heart

_____
_____
_____
_____
_____
_____
_____
_____
_____
_____
_____
_____
_____
_____
_____
_____
_____
_____
_____
_____

Date_____

Date_____

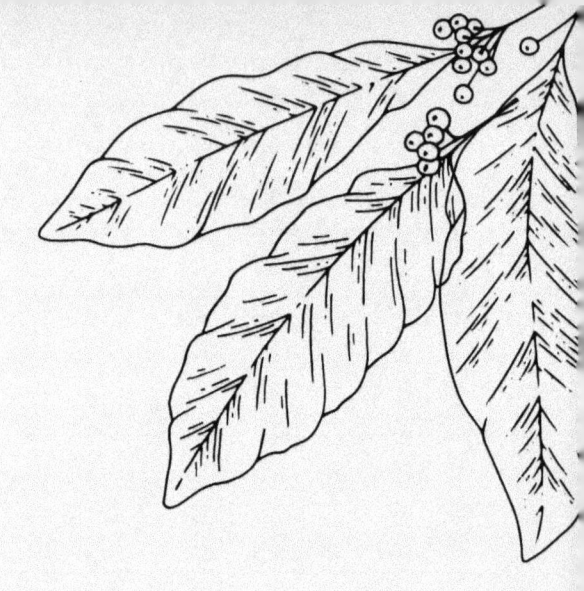

The Lord is near to all who call on him,
to all who call on him in truth.
Psalm 145:18

5 minute journaling

ONE THING I WANT TO THINK/REMEMBER ABOUT TODAY...

_____
_____
_____
_____
_____

PRAYER REQUESTS AND ANSWERS

_____
_____
_____
_____
_____

TODAY I'M GRATEFUL FOR...

_____
_____
_____
_____
_____

Date_____

5 minute journaling

ONE THING I WANT TO THINK/REMEMBER ABOUT TODAY...

___

PRAYER REQUESTS AND ANSWERS

___

TODAY I'M GRATEFUL FOR...

___

Date_____

5 minute journaling

ONE THING I WANT TO THINK/REMEMBER ABOUT TODAY...

_____

_____

_____

_____

_____

PRAYER REQUESTS AND ANSWERS

_____

_____

_____

_____

_____

TODAY I'M GRATEFUL FOR...

_____

_____

_____

_____

_____

_____

Date_____

ONE THING I WANT TO THINK/REMEMBER ABOUT TODAY...

_____
_____
_____
_____
_____

PRAYER REQUESTS AND ANSWERS

_____
_____
_____
_____
_____

TODAY I'M GRATEFUL FOR...

_____
_____
_____
_____
_____

Date_____

5 minute journaling

ONE THING I WANT TO THINK/REMEMBER ABOUT TODAY...

_____
_____
_____
_____
_____
_____

PRAYER REQUESTS AND ANSWERS

_____
_____
_____
_____
_____
_____

TODAY I'M GRATEFUL FOR...

_____
_____
_____
_____
_____
_____

Date_____

What's on your heart

Date_____

Date_____

I urge, then, first of all, that petitions,
prayers, intercession and thanksgiving
be made for all people—
for kings and all those in authority,
that we may live peaceful and quiet
lives in all godliness and holiness.
1 Timothy 2:1-2

5 minute journaling

ONE THING I WANT TO THINK/REMEMBER ABOUT TODAY...

___

PRAYER REQUESTS AND ANSWERS

___

TODAY I'M GRATEFUL FOR...

___

Date_____

5 minute journaling

ONE THING I WANT TO THINK/REMEMBER ABOUT TODAY...

_____
_____
_____
_____
_____
_____

PRAYER REQUESTS AND ANSWERS

_____
_____
_____
_____
_____
_____

TODAY I'M GRATEFUL FOR...

_____
_____
_____
_____
_____
_____

Date_____

# 5 minute journaling

ONE THING I WANT TO THINK/REMEMBER ABOUT TODAY...

_____
_____
_____
_____
_____

PRAYER REQUESTS AND ANSWERS

_____
_____
_____
_____
_____

TODAY I'M GRATEFUL FOR...

_____
_____
_____
_____
_____

Date_____

5 minute journaling

ONE THING I WANT TO THINK/REMEMBER ABOUT TODAY...

_____
_____
_____
_____
_____

PRAYER REQUESTS AND ANSWERS

_____
_____
_____
_____
_____

TODAY I'M GRATEFUL FOR...

_____
_____
_____
_____
_____

Date_____

5 minute journaling

ONE THING I WANT TO THINK/REMEMBER ABOUT TODAY...

_____
_____
_____
_____
_____

PRAYER REQUESTS AND ANSWERS

_____
_____
_____
_____
_____

TODAY I'M GRATEFUL FOR...

_____
_____
_____
_____
_____

Date_____

What's on your heart

_____

_____

_____

_____

_____

_____

_____

_____

_____

_____

_____

_____

_____

_____

_____

_____

_____

_____

Date_____

Date_____

For where two or three gather in my name, there am I with them.

Matthew 18:20

5 minute journaling

ONE THING I WANT TO THINK/REMEMBER ABOUT TODAY...

_____
_____
_____
_____
_____

PRAYER REQUESTS AND ANSWERS

_____
_____
_____
_____
_____

TODAY I'M GRATEFUL FOR...

_____
_____
_____
_____
_____

Date_____

5 minute journaling

ONE THING I WANT TO THINK/REMEMBER ABOUT TODAY...

_____
_____
_____
_____
_____

PRAYER REQUESTS AND ANSWERS

_____
_____
_____
_____
_____

TODAY I'M GRATEFUL FOR...

_____
_____
_____
_____
_____

Date_____

5 minute journaling

ONE THING I WANT TO THINK/REMEMBER ABOUT TODAY...

_____
_____
_____
_____
_____
_____

PRAYER REQUESTS AND ANSWERS

_____
_____
_____
_____
_____
_____

TODAY I'M GRATEFUL FOR...

_____
_____
_____
_____
_____
_____

Date_____

5 minute journaling

ONE THING I WANT TO THINK/REMEMBER ABOUT TODAY...

_____
_____
_____
_____
_____

PRAYER REQUESTS AND ANSWERS

_____
_____
_____
_____
_____

TODAY I'M GRATEFUL FOR...

_____
_____
_____
_____
_____

Date_____

5 minute journaling

ONE THING I WANT TO THINK/REMEMBER ABOUT TODAY...

_____
_____
_____
_____
_____
_____

PRAYER REQUESTS AND ANSWERS

_____
_____
_____
_____
_____
_____

TODAY I'M GRATEFUL FOR...

_____
_____
_____
_____
_____
_____

Date_____

What's on your heart

Date_____

Date_____

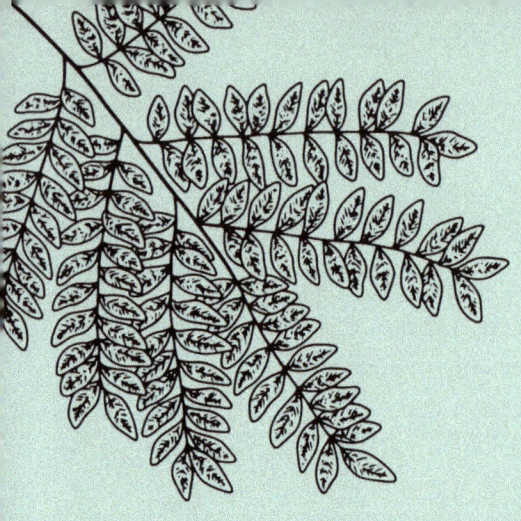

Let us then approach God's throne of grace with confidence, so that we may receive mercy and find grace to help us in our time of need.
Hebrews 4:16

ONE THING I WANT TO THINK/REMEMBER ABOUT TODAY…

_____
_____
_____
_____
_____
_____

PRAYER REQUESTS AND ANSWERS

_____
_____
_____
_____
_____
_____

TODAY I'M GRATEFUL FOR…

_____
_____
_____
_____
_____
_____

Date_____

5 minute journaling

ONE THING I WANT TO THINK/REMEMBER ABOUT TODAY...

_____
_____
_____
_____
_____

PRAYER REQUESTS AND ANSWERS

_____
_____
_____
_____
_____

TODAY I'M GRATEFUL FOR...

_____
_____
_____
_____
_____

Date_____

5 minute journaling

ONE THING I WANT TO THINK/REMEMBER ABOUT TODAY...

_____
_____
_____
_____
_____
_____

PRAYER REQUESTS AND ANSWERS

_____
_____
_____
_____
_____
_____

TODAY I'M GRATEFUL FOR...

_____
_____
_____
_____
_____
_____

Date_____

5 minute journaling

ONE THING I WANT TO THINK/REMEMBER ABOUT TODAY...

_____
_____
_____
_____
_____

PRAYER REQUESTS AND ANSWERS

_____
_____
_____
_____
_____

TODAY I'M GRATEFUL FOR...

_____
_____
_____
_____
_____

Date_____

5 minute journaling

ONE THING I WANT TO THINK/REMEMBER ABOUT TODAY...

_____
_____
_____
_____
_____
_____

PRAYER REQUESTS AND ANSWERS

_____
_____
_____
_____
_____
_____

TODAY I'M GRATEFUL FOR...

_____
_____
_____
_____
_____
_____

Date_____

What's on your heart

Date_____

Date_____

Be joyful in hope, patient in affliction, faithful in prayer.

Romans 12:12

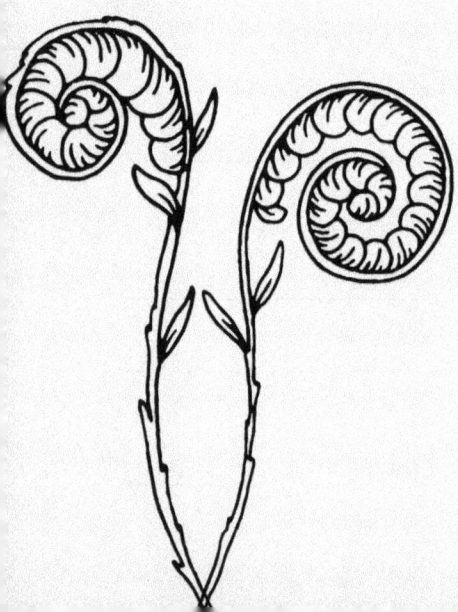

5 minute journaling

ONE THING I WANT TO THINK/REMEMBER ABOUT TODAY...

_____
_____
_____
_____
_____
_____

PRAYER REQUESTS AND ANSWERS

_____
_____
_____
_____
_____
_____

TODAY I'M GRATEFUL FOR...

_____
_____
_____
_____
_____
_____

Date_____

ONE THING I WANT TO THINK/REMEMBER ABOUT TODAY...
_____
_____
_____
_____
_____

PRAYER REQUESTS AND ANSWERS
_____
_____
_____
_____
_____

TODAY I'M GRATEFUL FOR...
_____
_____
_____
_____
_____

Date_____

5 minute journaling

ONE THING I WANT TO THINK/REMEMBER ABOUT TODAY...

_____
_____
_____
_____
_____

PRAYER REQUESTS AND ANSWERS

_____
_____
_____
_____
_____

TODAY I'M GRATEFUL FOR...

_____
_____
_____
_____
_____

Date_____

5 minute journaling

ONE THING I WANT TO THINK/REMEMBER ABOUT TODAY...

_____
_____
_____
_____
_____

PRAYER REQUESTS AND ANSWERS

_____
_____
_____
_____
_____

TODAY I'M GRATEFUL FOR...

_____
_____
_____
_____
_____

Date_____

5 minute journaling

ONE THING I WANT TO THINK/REMEMBER ABOUT TODAY...

_____
_____
_____
_____
_____
_____

PRAYER REQUESTS AND ANSWERS

_____
_____
_____
_____
_____
_____

TODAY I'M GRATEFUL FOR...

_____
_____
_____
_____
_____
_____

Date_____

What's on your heart

Date_____

Date_____

But when you ask, you must believe and not doubt, because the one who doubts is like a wave of the sea, blown and tossed by the wind.

James 1:6

ONE THING I WANT TO THINK/REMEMBER ABOUT TODAY...

PRAYER REQUESTS AND ANSWERS

TODAY I'M GRATEFUL FOR...

Date_____

5 minute journaling

ONE THING I WANT TO THINK/REMEMBER ABOUT TODAY...

_____
_____
_____
_____
_____

PRAYER REQUESTS AND ANSWERS

_____
_____
_____
_____
_____
_____

TODAY I'M GRATEFUL FOR...

_____
_____
_____
_____
_____

Date_____

ONE THING I WANT TO THINK/REMEMBER ABOUT TODAY...

_____
_____
_____
_____
_____

PRAYER REQUESTS AND ANSWERS

_____
_____
_____
_____
_____

TODAY I'M GRATEFUL FOR...

_____
_____
_____
_____
_____

Date_____

5 minute journaling

ONE THING I WANT TO THINK/REMEMBER ABOUT TODAY...

___

___

___

___

___

___

PRAYER REQUESTS AND ANSWERS

___

___

___

___

___

___

TODAY I'M GRATEFUL FOR...

___

___

___

___

___

___

Date_____

5 minute journaling

ONE THING I WANT TO THINK/REMEMBER ABOUT TODAY...

___

PRAYER REQUESTS AND ANSWERS

___

TODAY I'M GRATEFUL FOR...

___

Date_____

What's on your heart

Date_____

Date_____

I cried out to him with my mouth,
his praise was on my tongue.
Psalm 66:17

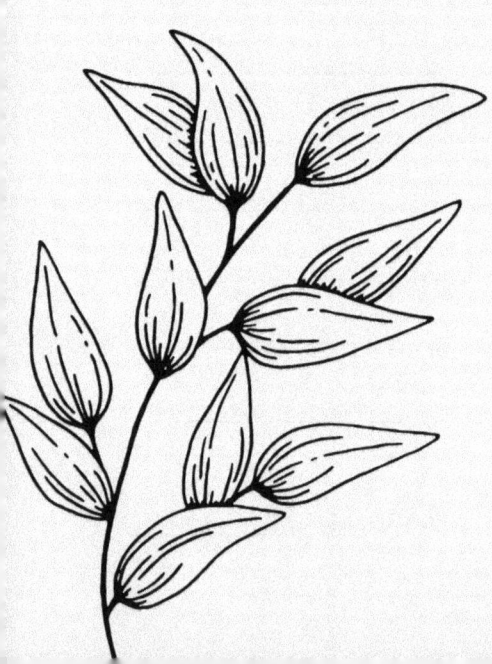

5 minute journaling

ONE THING I WANT TO THINK/REMEMBER ABOUT TODAY...

_____
_____
_____
_____
_____
_____

PRAYER REQUESTS AND ANSWERS

_____
_____
_____
_____
_____
_____

TODAY I'M GRATEFUL FOR...

_____
_____
_____
_____
_____
_____

Date_____

5 minute journaling

ONE THING I WANT TO THINK/REMEMBER ABOUT TODAY...

_____
_____
_____
_____
_____

PRAYER REQUESTS AND ANSWERS

_____
_____
_____
_____
_____

TODAY I'M GRATEFUL FOR...

_____
_____
_____
_____
_____

Date_____

5 minute journaling

ONE THING I WANT TO THINK/REMEMBER ABOUT TODAY...

_____
_____
_____
_____
_____
_____

PRAYER REQUESTS AND ANSWERS

_____
_____
_____
_____
_____
_____

TODAY I'M GRATEFUL FOR...

_____
_____
_____
_____
_____
_____

Date_____

ONE THING I WANT TO THINK/REMEMBER ABOUT TODAY...

_____
_____
_____
_____
_____

PRAYER REQUESTS AND ANSWERS

_____
_____
_____
_____
_____
_____

TODAY I'M GRATEFUL FOR...

_____
_____
_____
_____
_____

Date_____

5 minute journaling

ONE THING I WANT TO THINK/REMEMBER ABOUT TODAY...

_____
_____
_____
_____
_____

PRAYER REQUESTS AND ANSWERS

_____
_____
_____
_____
_____

TODAY I'M GRATEFUL FOR...

_____
_____
_____
_____
_____

Date_____

What's on your heart

Date_____

Date_____

In the morning, Lord, you hear my voice, in the morning I lay my requests before you and wait expectantly.
Psalm 5:3

5 minute journaling

ONE THING I WANT TO THINK/REMEMBER ABOUT TODAY...

_____
_____
_____
_____
_____

PRAYER REQUESTS AND ANSWERS

_____
_____
_____
_____
_____

TODAY I'M GRATEFUL FOR...

_____
_____
_____
_____
_____

Date_____

5 minute journaling

ONE THING I WANT TO THINK/REMEMBER ABOUT TODAY...

___

PRAYER REQUESTS AND ANSWERS

___

TODAY I'M GRATEFUL FOR...

___

Date_____

5 minute journaling

ONE THING I WANT TO THINK/REMEMBER ABOUT TODAY...

_____
_____
_____
_____
_____

PRAYER REQUESTS AND ANSWERS

_____
_____
_____
_____
_____

TODAY I'M GRATEFUL FOR...

_____
_____
_____
_____
_____

Date_____

5 minute journaling

ONE THING I WANT TO THINK/REMEMBER ABOUT TODAY...

_____
_____
_____
_____
_____

PRAYER REQUESTS AND ANSWERS

_____
_____
_____
_____
_____

TODAY I'M GRATEFUL FOR...

_____
_____
_____
_____
_____

Date_____

5 minute journaling

ONE THING I WANT TO THINK/REMEMBER ABOUT TODAY...

_____
_____
_____
_____
_____
_____

PRAYER REQUESTS AND ANSWERS

_____
_____
_____
_____
_____
_____

TODAY I'M GRATEFUL FOR...

_____
_____
_____
_____
_____
_____

Date_____

What's on your heart

_____
_____
_____
_____
_____
_____
_____
_____
_____
_____
_____
_____
_____
_____
_____
_____
_____

Date_____

Date_____

For I know that through your prayers and God's provision of the Spirit of Jesus Christ what has happened to me will turn out for my deliverance.

Philippians 1:19

5 minute journaling

ONE THING I WANT TO THINK/REMEMBER ABOUT TODAY...

PRAYER REQUESTS AND ANSWERS

TODAY I'M GRATEFUL FOR...

Date_____

5 minute journaling

ONE THING I WANT TO THINK/REMEMBER ABOUT TODAY...

_____
_____
_____
_____
_____

PRAYER REQUESTS AND ANSWERS

_____
_____
_____
_____
_____

TODAY I'M GRATEFUL FOR...

_____
_____
_____
_____
_____

Date_____

5 minute journaling

ONE THING I WANT TO THINK/REMEMBER ABOUT TODAY...

_____
_____
_____
_____
_____
_____

PRAYER REQUESTS AND ANSWERS

_____
_____
_____
_____
_____
_____

TODAY I'M GRATEFUL FOR...

_____
_____
_____
_____
_____
_____

Date_____

ONE THING I WANT TO THINK/REMEMBER ABOUT TODAY...

_____
_____
_____
_____
_____

PRAYER REQUESTS AND ANSWERS

_____
_____
_____
_____
_____

TODAY I'M GRATEFUL FOR...

_____
_____
_____
_____
_____

Date_____

5 minute journaling

ONE THING I WANT TO THINK/REMEMBER ABOUT TODAY...

_____
_____
_____
_____
_____
_____

PRAYER REQUESTS AND ANSWERS

_____
_____
_____
_____
_____
_____

TODAY I'M GRATEFUL FOR...

_____
_____
_____
_____
_____
_____

Date_____

What's on your heart

Date_____

Date_____

Dear friend, I pray that you may enjoy good health and that all may go well with you, even as your soul is getting along well.
3 John 1:2

www.ingramcontent.com/pod-product-compliance
Lightning Source LLC
Chambersburg PA
CBHW061137010526
44107CB00069B/2969